W9-CNF-313

Profiles in American History

The Life and Times of

ROSA PARKS

Mitchell Lane
PUBLISHERS

P.O. Box 196 · Hockessin, Delaware 19707

Titles in the Series

The Life and Times of

ROSA PARKS

Kathleen Tracy

Copyright © 2009 by Mitchell Lane Publishers, Inc. All rights reserved. No part of this book may be reproduced without written permission from the publisher. Printed and bound in the United States of America.

Printing   2   3   4   5   6   7   8   9

Library of Congress Cataloging-in-Publication Data
Tracy, Kathleen.
  The life and times of Rosa Parks / by Kathleen Tracy.
     p. cm.—(Profiles in American history)
  Includes bibliographical references and index.
  ISBN 978-1-58415-666-6 (library bound)
  1. Parks, Rosa, 1913-2005—Juvenile literature. 2. African American women—Alabama—Montgomery—Biography—Juvenile literature. 3. African Americans—Alabama—Montgomery—Biography—Juvenile literature. 4. Civil rights workers—Alabama—Montgomery—Biography—Juvenile literature. 5. African Americans—Civil rights—Alabama—Montgomery—History—20th century—Juvenile literature.
  6. Montgomery Bus Boycott, Montgomery, Ala., 1955–1956—Juvenile literature.
  7. Segregation in transportation—Alabama—Montgomery—History—20th century—Juvenile literature. 8. Montgomery (Ala.)—Race relations—History—20th century—Juvenile literature. 9. Montgomery (Ala.)—Biography—Juvenile literature. I. Title.
  F334.M753P3885 2009
  323.092—dc22
  [B]
                                                                                                        2008020927

ABOUT THE AUTHOR: Kathleen Tracy has been a journalist for over twenty years. Her writing has been featured in magazines including *The Toronto Star's Star Week, A&E Biography* magazine, *KidScreen* and *TV Times.* She is also the author of numerous books for Mitchell Lane Publishers, including *William Hewlett: Pioneer of the Computer Age; The Fall of the Berlin Wall; Leonardo da Vinci; The Story of September 11, 2001; Johnny Depp; Mariah Carey;* and *Kelly Clarkson.*

PUBLISHER'S NOTE: This story is based on the author's extensive research, which she believes to be accurate. Documentation of such research is contained on page 45.
     The internet sites referenced herein were active as of the publication date. Due to the fleeting nature of some web sites, we cannot guarantee they will all be active when you are reading this book.

PLB / PLB4

Contents

    *For Your Information

On December 1, 1955, Rosa Parks was arrested and charged with "refusing to obey orders of bus driver." While Rosa was in custody, her family feared for her safety: Defying Montgomery's long-standing segregation laws was dangerous.

CHAPTER
1

Tired

City officials in Montgomery, Alabama, were desperate. In the aftermath of Rosa Parks's arrest and conviction for not giving up her bus seat for white passengers, the city's black community began a boycott of city buses. What was supposed to be a one-day protest had turned into an ongoing battle of wills that was threatening to bankrupt the transportation system.

Parks was deeply involved in the boycott. While church leaders such as Martin Luther King Jr. and Ralph Abernathy negotiated with the mayor and other officials, Parks and other activists worked behind the scenes coordinating car pools and rides for black commuters. At first, black-owned cab companies offered rides for just ten cents, until the Montgomery police commissioner invoked an old statute requiring a minimum fare of forty-five cents. When that didn't quell the boycott, police officers began a campaign of harassment. People waiting for car-pool rides were arrested for loitering. Car-pool drivers were ticketed for driving too slow or for having old windshield wipers or for going one mile an hour over the posted speed limit. Martin Luther King himself was arrested and taken to the city jail for allegedly going 30 mph in a 25 mph zone. Still, the boycott continued.

Using an antiquated Montgomery law that prohibited boycotts without just cause, a grand jury indicted Dr. King and eighty-nine

others, including Rosa Parks and prominent community leader E.D. Nixon, for conspiring to conduct the bus boycott and interfering with private enterprise. They were arrested on February 22, 1956, booked, and released. The news of Parks's second arrest brought increased national attention to the situation in Montgomery and strengthened the resolve of the protesters. On March 19, Dr. King was the first to be tried. After a four-day trial, the presiding judge found King guilty of conducting an illegal boycott against Montgomery City Lines. He was fined $500 plus court costs, but the judge later suspended the sentence and postponed the remaining boycott cases while King's lawyers appealed the judgment.

Through it all, the boycott dragged on. Looking back, it is clear that city officials underestimated the resolve of Montgomery's black community, which was fueled in part by ongoing anger over the 1955 murder of a young man named Emmett Till, in the neighboring state of Mississippi.

It was a brutal crime that shocked many. It also brought the fundamental issues of the civil rights movement to the forefront of the American consciousness. Well into the 1950s, segregation in the Deep South was still rampant, as was resentment over the federal government's efforts to racially integrate their communities. Each small victory in the fight for racial equality stoked that bitterness into a simmering rage that frequently exploded into deadly violence. But what made the Till case so riveting—and polarizing—was the murderers' lack of remorse and the white community's apathy over two of their neighbors literally getting away with murder.

In August 1955, Emmett Till, a fourteen-year-old from Chicago, was visiting his uncle Moses "Preacher" Wright in the Mississippi Delta. A sharecropper, Moses lived in an isolated rural area where blacks and whites lived separate and unequal lives. The dusty town was called Money. It consisted of a gas station, a post office, a school, and a handful of stores clustered together in the middle of the surrounding cotton fields.

One of those businesses was Bryant's Grocery and Meat Market, operated by white owners Roy and Carolyn Bryant. Carolyn, a petite twenty-one-year-old who stood just five feet tall and weighed 103 pounds, had dropped out of high school when she was seventeen and married Roy, who was in the army's 82nd Airborne Division.

After he was discharged, Roy's brothers helped him set up the grocery store that sold goods mostly to the local black field hands. By 1955, Roy and Carolyn had two young sons, aged three and two, and were struggling financially. They lived in the back of their store, unable to afford a television, much less a car. On the evenings they were able to borrow a car, Carolyn and Roy went to the local drive-in to see a movie, their toddlers asleep in the backseat. They blamed much of their money woes on a government program that provided food to blacks, negating the need to buy from the Bryants' store.

It was a difficult life but they relied on their faith, and family, to get by. Roy's mom had been married twice. With her first husband she had five sons, known as the Milam children. She had six more children, three boys and three girls, with her next husband. These were the Bryant children. All eleven children were boisterous and tight-knit. And they all resented blacks challenging white superiority, and resisted any movement that promoted civil rights.

To earn extra money, Roy frequently drove a truck for his brother, leaving Carolyn to run the store in his absence. The family made sure Carolyn was never alone when Roy was away by having one of her sisters-in-law at the store with her. Since Carolyn was not allowed to sleep in the store alone overnight—nor were the women allowed to travel after dark unless accompanied by a man—one of Roy's brothers would pick up Carolyn and whoever was keeping her company and take them to his house.

On Wednesday, August 24, 1955, Roy was away on a run. That night, Carolyn's sister-in-law Juanita Milam, along with her two young sons, was at the store. Juanita's husband, J.W. Milam, was scheduled to pick them up after the store closed at nine o'clock.

About an hour and a half before closing time, eight young black youths—one girl and seven boys—pulled up outside the store in a 1946 Ford. The boys, aged thirteen to nineteen, were all related to Preacher Wright. Four of the young men lived in the area; the others, including Emmett "Bobo" Till, were visiting the Delta from Chicago. Although Till was just five feet five inches tall, he was stocky and muscular, weighing about 160 pounds. According to Preacher Wright, Bobo "looked like a man."[1]

The kids from the Ford joined another group of black youths who were already hanging out in front of the store. Roy Bryant

had installed checkerboards, and several of the teens were playing checkers while others talked or just fooled around. At some point, the boys began teasing each other about girls. Bobo boasted that he had a white girlfriend back in Chicago. To prove it, he showed everyone the picture of her he carried in his wallet. He also bragged that he and the girl were physically intimate.

One of the boys dared Bobo to show them just how good he was with white women by going into the store and asking Carolyn out on a date. At first, Bobo thought better of it. But when another one of the boys accused him of being afraid, he sauntered into the store by

Mamie Mobley-Till tried to warn her son, Emmett Till, that race relations in the South were different than they were in Chicago. Lynchings of African Americans were common in the South. Mamie would later refer to her son as the sacrificial lamb of the American civil rights movement.

himself, stopped near the candy display, and asked Carolyn for two cents' worth of bubble gum. When she held it out, Bobo squeezed her hand and reportedly asked her for a date.

When she yanked her hand away and started moving back, he allegedly stepped in front of her and said: "You needn't be afraid o' me, Baby. I been with white girls before."[2]

Those raised in the Delta quickly realized Bobo had gone way too far. A cousin ran inside the store and dragged Bobo out. Carolyn followed, running to Juanita's car—where she knew a gun was hidden under the front seat. As she ran past, Bobo gave her a "wolf whistle" before being pushed into another car and driven away.

Although frightened and upset, Carolyn agreed with Juanita that it was best they not tell their husbands what had happened. When J.W. came to pick them up, they did not mention the incident. However, the black youths weren't nearly so discreet. When Roy got back home on Friday and came to the store, one of his black customers mentioned that word was going around about a Chicago boy who had disrespected Carolyn. Roy confronted her, and she told him what had happened.

Some people would later claim that Roy had no choice but to confront Bobo; otherwise he would look like a coward to all his white neighbors. When J.W. stopped by on Saturday night, Roy explained the situation, and J.W. agreed to pick him up early Sunday morning to drive out to Preacher Wright's place.

At six feet two and 235 pounds, J.W., also called Big Milam, was an imposing figure. Although he had only a ninth-grade education, he had excelled in the army during World War II. He was a platoon leader and an expert in hand-to-hand combat. He survived several injuries, including shrapnel wounds and a bullet in the chest. When discharged, he kept his army Colt .45 automatic pistol.

Rather than waiting until morning to confront Bobo, J.W. woke Roy up at 2:00 a.m. They headed to Preacher's, which was a few miles outside of Money.

All of Bobo's cockiness was gone. He was terrified. He had wanted to go home to Chicago on Thursday, but Preacher's wife thought those people saying that Roy would kill Bobo were just being dramatic. Likewise, Preacher wasn't especially worried, and he brought Bobo out to confront Roy and J.W. However, when the

On September 19, 1955, Roy Bryant (left) and J.W. Milam stood trial for Emmett Till's murder. The two were acquitted.

two men ordered Bobo to lie in the back of the truck and drove off, the Wrights became fearful and contacted the sheriff.

Later, J.W. would say they intended only to pistol-whip Bobo and frighten him, but Bobo refused to be intimidated. No matter how many times Milam struck him with his Colt pistol, Bobo kept repeating that he was not afraid; he was as good as they were; and yes, he had been with white women.

"Well, what else could we do?" J.W. asked later. "I'm no bully; I never hurt a n*****s in my life. I like n*****s—in their place. . . . N*****s ain't gonna vote where I live. . . . They ain't gonna go to school with my kids. And when a n***** gets close to mentioning sex with a white woman, he's tired o' living. . . ."[3]

They drove Bobo to the Tallahatchie River, made him strip, and shot him. They tied a gin fan around his neck and threw his body into the river. Three days later, it was discovered by some young boys fishing.

J.W. Milam and Roy Bryant admitted in a *Look* magazine interview that they killed Emmett Till. But a jury in Sumner, Mississippi, after one hour of deliberation, found them not guilty of murder. Two months later, a grand jury declined to indict them for kidnapping.

The murder of Emmett Till became a rallying cry for the then-struggling civil rights movement. It inspired more blacks to become politically and socially active—including Rosa Parks.

E.D. Nixon

The Montgomery bus boycott helped end segregation in the South and made the Reverend Martin Luther King Jr. a national civil rights figure—yet without the behind-the-scenes efforts of union leader and civil rights activist E.D. Nixon, the boycott may have never happened.

Edgar Daniel Nixon was born in Montgomery, Alabama, on July 12, 1899. He was hired to work in the

E.D. Nixon (left) and his son, E.D. Nixon Jr.

baggage room of the local train station and worked his way up to Pullman car porter, a job similar to a hotel concierge, where he would assist passengers with their individual needs. Despite having gone to school for only a little more than a year, Nixon was street-smart and interested in politics. He formed the state branch of the Brotherhood of Sleeping Car Porters (the first union controlled by blacks) and served as its president for twenty-five years. In 1944, he was elected president of the Voters League of Montgomery and later was appointed head of the Montgomery chapter of the National Association for the Advancement of Colored People (NAACP). There he met Rosa Parks, who worked as the group's secretary.

After Parks's arrest, it was Nixon who helped bail her out of jail and convinced her to use her arrest to challenge Montgomery's segregated bus system. As soon as Parks agreed, Nixon worked with the Women's Political Council to organize the boycott. He then asked the new pastor at Dexter Avenue Baptist Church, Martin Luther King Jr., if he would host a meeting at his church to discuss the boycott. At that meeting, Nixon nominated King to serve as president of the newly launched Montgomery Improvement Association (MIA) and publicly lead the boycott.

While Nixon was gratified with the boycott's success, he reportedly became increasingly resentful over how much credit Reverend King received for the boycott and how much public attention he received in the following years. Tensions between the two civil rights leaders increased and led to Nixon's resignation in 1957 from the MIA, although he publicly maintained his admiration for King's work.

Nixon remained a civil rights activist the rest of his life, dedicating his later years to improving living conditions at housing projects and establishing programs for minority youths. He died in Montgomery on February 25, 1987.

For Your Information

A teenage Rosa and her friend Samson Smith. Rosa's mother saved for years to send her daughter to school. Although Montgomery had free public schools, they were for white children only. Rosa attended Alabama State College for Negroes for her sophomore and junior years but had to drop out to take care of her grandmother.

CHAPTER
2

Growing Up Segregated

Rosa Louise McCauley was born on February 4, 1913, in Tuskegee, Alabama. Her father, James, worked as a carpenter, and her mother, Leona Edwards McCauley, was a teacher. Rosa's brother, Sylvester, was born two years later, and not long afterward Leona and James separated. Leona took Rosa and Sylvester to her parents' farm in Pine Level, Alabama. Rosa, who was named for her maternal grandmother, Rose Edwards, remembered being taught to read by her mother at a very young age. "I liked to read all sorts of stories, like fairy tales—*Little Red Riding Hood, Mother Goose. . . .* I read very often."[1]

Rosa attended a small, rural one-room school for blacks that enrolled about sixty students in grades one through six. Leona was one of the teachers there, and Rosa's first teacher was Miss Sally Hill. Rosa enjoyed school, but she and the other students attended class only five months out of the year so that the children would be available the rest of the time to help work on local farms. "The parents had to buy whatever the student used," Rosa recalled. "Often, if your family couldn't afford it, you had no access to books, pencils, whatever. However, often the children would share."[2]

Even as a child, Rosa was aware that black people were treated less fairly than whites, but she didn't understand why. "But when I did learn about it, I didn't feel very good about it."[3]

Rosa remembered lying in her bed late at night and hearing members of the Ku Klux Klan ride by her house, worrying that they

would burn it down. At times, the frightening sounds of black men being lynched cut through the stillness. Rosa said her mother and grandparents instilled in her the belief that it was important to stand up for what you believe, regardless of the potential consequences.

"My mother was a teacher in a little school," Rosa told the Academy of Achievement in 1995, "and she believed in freedom and equality for people, and did not have the notion that we were supposed to live as we did, under legally enforced racial segregation. She didn't believe in it. . . . We were human beings and we should be treated as such."[4]

Rosa's grandparents were born before the Civil War and grew up as slaves. "They suffered a lot as children and of course, after slavery [their life] was not that much better. . . . They were farmers in a rural area in Alabama."[5]

In 1924, Leona enrolled eleven-year-old Rosa in the Montgomery Industrial School for Girls. It was also known as Miss White's School for Girls. A private school, it had been founded by liberal-thinking Northern women who stressed the importance of self-worth. It was a philosophy that Leona embraced and tried to instill in her daughter. In an interview with the Academy of Achievement, Rosa recalled her mother telling her to "take advantage of the opportunities, no matter how few they were."[6]

In Montgomery, Alabama, during the 1920s, opportunities were indeed scarce for blacks in general, and even more so for black women. "During my growing up there, it was completely legally enforced racial segregation, and of course, I struggled against it for a long time," Rosa later said. "I felt that it was not right to be deprived of freedom when we were living in the Home of the Brave and Land of the Free."[7]

Mrs. Parks also recalled in an interview, "Back then we didn't have any civil rights. It was just a matter of survival, of existing from one day to the next."[8]

After completing her studies at Miss White's, where she had cleaned classrooms to help pay her tuition, Rosa attended high school at the Alabama State Teachers College. She had to drop out before graduating in order to help care for her dying grandmother, Rose. Then, just as Rosa was ready to return to high school, Leona fell ill.

After the Civil War, slavery was abolished, but blacks still had few opportunities. The end of slavery transformed the social system of the South.

Rosa again put off her education to tend to her mother and take care of the house, while Sylvester worked to support the family.

When she was nineteen, mutual friends introduced Rosa to a barber named Raymond Parks. Although Raymond did not have a formal education, he was self-taught and was particularly knowledgeable about current events and domestic politics. His intellect was so sharp that most people who met him believed he was college-educated. Throughout his life, Raymond promoted the importance of education to young people.

At first, Rosa and Raymond were just friends. Although Raymond was very handsome, charming, and well dressed, Rosa later admitted in interviews that she was not romantically attracted to him because he was so light-skinned. But as their friendship deepened, her attraction grew. Plus, she would later say, Raymond's persistence wore down her resistance.

On December 18, 1932, Rosa and Raymond were married at Leona's house in Montgomery. Rosa was nineteen and Raymond was twenty-nine. With his support, Rosa finally earned her high school diploma two years later and they settled in Montgomery. They became members of an African Methodist Episcopal (AME) church, and together they worked for the city's chapter of the NAACP.

"I worked on numerous cases with the NAACP," Parks recalled, "but we did not get the publicity. There were cases of flogging,

peonage, murder, and rape. We didn't seem to have too many successes. It was more a matter of trying to challenge the powers that be, and to let it be known that we did not wish to continue being second-class citizens."9

Over the next many years, Rosa and Raymond worked quietly behind the scenes to better the lives of blacks in Montgomery and the rest of the South. Rosa served as secretary of the NAACP and was later an adviser to the NAACP Youth Council, which educates young blacks about problems facing blacks and other minorities. Every day she and other blacks continued to face bigotry and inequality. It was a struggle for them to register to vote, and on an almost daily basis black bus riders were thrown off by white drivers for not following segregation laws.

The laws in Montgomery required blacks to get on the bus at the front to pay their fare to the driver, then get off and reboard through the back door. It wasn't unusual for the bus to drive off before the paid-up customers made it to the back entrance. If the white section was full, blacks were required to give up their seats and move farther to the back if another white rider got on. Blacks were not even allowed to sit across the aisle from whites. What made the situation especially insulting was that two-thirds of the bus riders in Montgomery were black.

Parks recalled the humiliation of once being tossed off a bus: "I didn't want to pay my fare and then go around the back door, because many times, even if you did that, you might not get on the bus at all. They'd probably shut the door, drive off, and leave you standing there."10

So it was particularly fitting that when Rosa decided to make a personal statement and take a stand against a lifetime of bigotry, she did it on a bus.

Cleveland Avenue bus that Parks was riding on December 1, 1955.

The Ku Klux Klan

Klansmen under arrest

The Ku Klux Klan is a white supremacy organization. It was originally established in 1866 by veterans of the Confederate army who opposed Reconstruction and carpetbaggers—Northern opportunists who moved South to make money from post–Civil War rebuilding. They were also intent on keeping the newly freed slaves "in their place." The first Grand Wizard or head of the Ku Klux Klan was former Confederate general Nathan Forrest. Klansmen wearing masks and draped in white sheets tortured and killed blacks and sympathetic whites. They also targeted immigrants. But many Southerners believed the Klan's methods simply brought more governmental scrutiny and gave the North an excuse to keep their troops in the South. Without the support of the Southern elite, the Klan's influence quickly declined and by the 1870s was effectively broken up by the Civil Rights Act of 1871, also known as the Ku Klux Klan Act.

Then in November 1915, a new group formed that used the same name, in honor of those Civil War veterans depicted in the film *The Birth of a Nation*. On Thanksgiving night, William Joseph Simmons and thirty-three others burned a cross on Stone Mountain, Georgia, while reading from the Bible. That night, he declared the founding of the new Knights of the Ku Klux Klan.

The new Klan was more organized than the original and established chapters across the country. At the height of its power in the early 1920s, it is estimated that up to five million men were members. This Klan not only preached white supremacy, they were also against Jews, Catholics, homosexuals, and Communists. The Klan's popularity began to wane during the Depression, and its membership dwindled during World War II because of its support for Hitler's Nazis. In the 1950s and 1960s, several independent groups adopted the Klan moniker while fighting against the civil rights movement.

In 2008, there were approximately 150 Klan chapters nationwide, with up to 8,000 members. Widely considered an extremist hate group, the Klan has been renounced by all mainstream politicians and religious leaders.

For Your Information

Rosa Parks was not the first person to be arrested for violating the segregation laws on the city buses in Montgomery, but she was chosen to be the one to challenge the law because of her well-regarded character and because she was active in the Montgomery chapter of the NAACP.

CHAPTER
3

Birth of an Activist

It was an act of civil disobedience that would reverberate through the entire country. It was dark at 6:00 P.M. on Thursday, December 1, 1955, when Rosa Parks left the Montgomery Fair department store where she worked as a seamstress. Even though it had been a long day, she wasn't particularly tired. Nor, as some reports would later suggest, were her feet tired. She boarded the Cleveland Avenue bus and immediately recognized the driver, James Blake, as the one who had kicked her off a bus twelve years earlier when she refused to reboard through the back door. Rosa paid her fare and sat in the fifth row, the first row of the "colored section."

By the third stop, the white section was full and several white passengers were standing. The bus driver demanded that Rosa and the other three riders sitting in her row get up so that the white passengers could sit down. The other three moved, but Rosa refused. As a paying bus rider, she felt she had the right to keep her seat. When the driver warned Parks that he would call the police if she didn't give up her seat, she politely told him to go ahead and contact the authorities. When officers Fletcher B. Day and Dempsey W. Mixon arrived, Rosa was arrested for violating the segregation laws of the City of Montgomery and the State of Alabama's Transportation Department.

Parks would later try to explain what had inspired her to choose that exact moment to defy the segregation laws. "The time had just come when I had been pushed as far as I could stand to be pushed, I suppose. They placed me under arrest. And I wasn't afraid. I don't know why I wasn't, but I didn't feel afraid. I had decided that I would have to know once and for all what rights I had as a human being and a citizen, even in Montgomery, Alabama."[1]

She added, "Our mistreatment was just not right, and I was tired of it. I kept thinking about my mother and my grandparents, and how strong they were. I knew there was a possibility of being mistreated, but an opportunity was being given to me to do what I had asked of others."[2]

Many people don't realize that Rosa was not the first person to get arrested for refusing to relinquish a seat on a Montgomery bus. She was, however, the perfect person to use to test the law. At the time of Parks's arrest, local black activists had decided to challenge Montgomery's segregation laws in court and had been looking for the right person to work with.

Eight months earlier, on March 2, a fifteen-year-old high school student named Claudette Colvin had been arrested after refusing to give up her seat to a white man. She was handcuffed and forcibly removed from the bus. Colvin was active in the NAACP's Youth Council. When Colvin was interviewed, Parks attended the meeting because she was secretary of the local NAACP chapter. In the end, the NAACP decided not to use Colvin when it was discovered she was pregnant. The activists felt they needed someone with community standing. They also needed someone who could withstand the stress of a court battle and the scrutiny of the press. An unwed teenaged mother was not the image they wanted to promote, neither to the media nor to the conservative black churches that would be asked to support whatever plaintiff was chosen. Plus, Colvin was rough around the edges and prone to angry outbursts and swearing. She was passed over, and her subsequent fine was paid without protest.

In October 1955, a young woman named Mary Louise Smith was arrested. Again, NAACP leaders rejected her, so Smith paid the fine and was released. Community activists were still waiting for the right moment on the fateful night Rosa stepped on the bus.

When E.D. Nixon, who was Rosa's boss at the NAACP, heard the news about her arrest, he is said to have exclaimed, "My God, look what segregation has put in my hands!"[3] Parks, then forty-two, was the perfect test case. She was married, employed, active in the community, and had enough personal fortitude to withstand the pressure that was sure to follow.

Rosa was bailed out shortly after being booked. Her bail was posted by Nixon, attorney Clifford Durr and his wife, Virginia. Clifford was a longtime civil rights activist who had once run for the U.S. Senate on a platform of equal rights for all citizens. The Durrs had employed Parks as a seamstress but also knew her through the NAACP. After it was agreed to make Rosa's arrest the test case, Nixon and other local activists organized their response. From the beginning, it was decided that the response to Parks's arrest must be nonviolent. "Being the minority, we felt that nothing could be gained by violence or threats or belligerent attitude," Parks explained. "We believed that more could be accomplished through the nonviolent passive resistance . . . and people just began to decide that they wouldn't ride the bus on the day of my trial,"[4] which would be held Monday, December 5, four days after her arrest. The Women's Political Council printed 35,000 flyers and distributed them Friday morning to all the black schools. The flyers called for a boycott:

> We are . . . asking every Negro to stay off the buses Monday in protest of the arrest and trial. . . . You can afford to stay out of school for one day. If you work, take a cab, or walk. But please, children and grown-ups, don't ride the bus at all on Monday. Please stay off the buses Monday.[5]

On Monday, the skies were overcast and there was a threat of rain, but the blacks of Montgomery stayed off the buses. Black-owned cabs offered rides for ten cents—the same price as one bus fare. A throng of spectators was waiting at the courthouse when Rosa Parks arrived. She walked slowly toward the entrance, looking dignified in a long-sleeved black dress with white cuffs and collar, a black velvet hat, a gray coat, and white gloves.

The trial lasted a half hour. As expected, Rosa was found guilty, but she refused to pay the $14 fine. Instead, her lawyers—Fred Gray and Charles Langford—filed an appeal to the conviction. This would give them a chance to challenge whether the law Rosa had broken was constitutional.

That same afternoon, the Montgomery Improvement Association was founded. The members elected the young minister of Dexter Avenue Baptist Church, Martin Luther King Jr., as its president. Parks had first met the charismatic preacher in August 1955. "He came to be a speaker at the NAACP meeting," she recalled. "I was very impressed not only with his youth but his very graceful and friendly manner and also his dedication to see that we have freedom for all people."[6]

That night, the twenty-six-year-old Reverend King addressed the crowd that had gathered at the Holt Street Baptist Church, saying, "There comes a time that people get tired."[7] Afterward, Parks stood up so that the audience could see her. The civil rights movement now had a face.

In the days after Rosa's arrest, several inaccurate stories were printed about the incident. One newspaper reported that Parks had sat in the white section and refused to move. Others suggested that she intentionally set out to get arrested, an accusation Parks firmly denied. "I did not get on the bus to get arrested," she said. "I got on the bus to go home."[8]

She also said, "I hadn't thought that I would be the person to do this. It hadn't occurred to me. Others had gone through the same experience, some even worse experience than mine."[9] She also denied a newspaper report that indicated she said her feet hurt and she was too tired to stand up.

Because the one-day boycott had been so successful, the MIA leaders decided it should continue until the segregation of the buses ended.

Rosa Parks statue in the Rosa Parks Museum in Alabama

Brown v. Board of Education

While the Civil War may have freed the slaves, it did nothing to assure African Americans they would be treated as equal citizens. Up until the mid-1950s, the South remained segregated, and this policy was upheld by the law. In 1896, the United States Supreme Court determined in *Plessy v. Ferguson* that as long as the separate facilities were "equal," the segregation did not violate the Fourteenth Amendment, which says that "no state shall . . . deny to any person . . . the equal protection of the laws."[10] Based on this decision, seventeen states enacted laws requiring racial segregation in their school systems.

In 1951, a class action suit was filed by thirteen parents on behalf of their twenty children against the Topeka, Kansas, Board of Education. Under an 1879 state law that permitted—but did not mandate—separate schools for blacks in communities with populations in excess of 15,000 people, Topeka's school district segregated its elementary schools.

As they would in Montgomery, local NAACP representatives recruited the parents willing to participate in the lawsuit. The named plaintiff, Oliver Brown, was a welder for the Santa Fe Railroad and an assistant pastor at his church. His daughter Linda was in third grade, and Brown had previously contacted a Topeka lawyer to discuss his concerns about "separate but equal." Instead of being able to attend the school a few blocks away from her family's house, Linda had to walk six blocks to the bus stop, then ride to the closest black school.

In 1954, Supreme Court Chief Justice Earl Warren wrote for the majority that "in the field of public education, the doctrine of 'separate but equal' has no place. Separate educational facilities are inherently unequal. Therefore, we hold that the plaintiffs are, by reason of the segregation complained of, deprived of the equal protection of the laws guaranteed by the Fourteenth Amendment."[11]

Linda Brown at age 9

Rosa at her sewing machine. After Rosa was arrested, she and her husband received numerous threats, including hate mail and harassing phone calls. Rosa also lost her job as a department store seamstress. Still, she would later say she was never afraid, just annoyed by the reaction.

CHAPTER
4

Fallout

After lawyers Fred Gray and Charles Langford filed Rosa's appeal, the case became tied up in the Alabama courts. While the wheels of justice turned slowly, Rosa felt the fallout from her actions.

"Very shortly after the boycott began, I was dismissed from my job as a seamstress at a department store," she later recalled. "I don't know why I was dismissed from the job, but I think it was because I was arrested. I worked at home doing sewing and typing."[1]

Raymond quit his job after his boss forbade him to talk about his wife or the legal case. Together Rosa and Raymond endured repeated verbal threats, harassing telephone calls, and hate mail, but Rosa faced the uncertainty in her typical stoic manner. In fact, from the moment she defied bus driver Blake, Rosa said she felt no fear. "I felt more annoyed than frightened. I was thinking mostly about how inconvenienced I was . . . stopping me from going home and doing my work—something I had not expected. I did not really know what would happen."[2]

What she did know was that things needed to change. "There were places black people couldn't go, and rights we did not have. This was not acceptable to me. A lot of other people didn't disobey the rules because they didn't want to get into trouble. I was willing to get arrested—it was worth the consequences. I don't think well of people who are prejudiced against people because of race,"[3] she

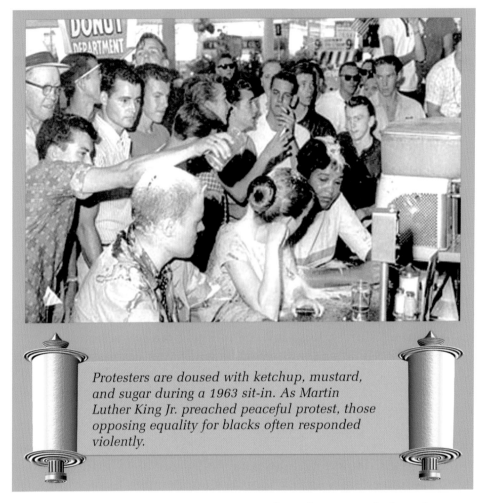

Protesters are doused with ketchup, mustard, and sugar during a 1963 sit-in. As Martin Luther King Jr. preached peaceful protest, those opposing equality for blacks often responded violently.

said. Then she added, "I never saw the Klansmen [when I was a child]. But I did know that they had gone through the community and mistreated people and drove them from their homes. I saw the results of what had happened. I do remember a young man who was found lying dead in the woods and nobody saw who had done it. . . .

"The only way for prejudiced people to change is for them to decide for themselves that all human beings should be treated fairly. We can't force them to think that way."[4]

Rosa looked to Raymond for support and encouragement. "He was the first, aside from my grandfather . . . who was never actually afraid of white people. So many African Americans felt that you

just had to be under Mr. Charlie's heel—that's what we called the white man, Mr. Charlie—and couldn't do anything to cross him. In other words, [Raymond] believed in being a man and expected to be treated as a man. . . . He believed in freedom and equality and all the things that would improve conditions."[5]

Rosa also found inspiration and solace in her faith. She noted, "I had a very spiritual background . . . I believe in church and my faith and that has helped to give me the strength and courage to live as I did."[6]

She also commented, "Usually, if I have to face something, I do so no matter what the consequences might be. I never had any desire to give up. I did not feel that giving up would be a way to become a free person. That's the way I still feel." However, she admitted, "By standing up to something we still don't always [effect] change right away. Even when we are brave and have courage, change still doesn't come about for a long time."[7]

That didn't keep others from moving forward. In addition to the bus boycott in Montgomery, Reverend King organized other protests demanding equal rights for all people. Thousands of people, black and white, participated in sit-ins and demonstrations in cities throughout the South.

Rosa later recalled that in addition to being impressed by King as a dynamic speaker, she was struck by "his genuine friendliness as a person. And his attitude, of course, was to work and do whatever he could in the community for the church to make a difference in the way of life we had at that time. He seemed to be a very genuine and very concerned person, and, I thought, a real Christian." It didn't surprise her that he became a national hero. "He was the type of person that people really gravitated towards and they seemed to like him personally, as well as his leadership."[8]

There is no argument that Rosa Parks's arrest for refusing to give up her seat on the bus was unquestionably the event that galvanized Montgomery's black community and prompted the successful boycott. But it was *Browder v. Gayle*, and not the Parks case, that led to the court decision to make segregation illegal.

Two months after the boycott was implemented, attorneys Clifford Durr, Fred Gray, and E.D. Nixon were still looking for a court case they could use to directly challenge Montgomery's bus segregation.

The problem with the Parks case was that it could be tied up in the appeals process for years. The activists did not want to wait that long for change. So, Fred Gray approached four other women who had been arrested or otherwise mistreated on the basis of the bus segregation laws—Aurelia Browder, a local housewife; Claudette Colvin; Susie McDonald; and Mary Louise Smith. They agreed to be plaintiffs in a civil action. On February 1, 1956, Gray filed the lawsuit *Browder v. Gayle* against the public transportation system, naming Montgomery's mayor, W. A. Gayle, as the defendant.

The legal question posed by the lawsuit was: Did racial segregation on Montgomery's self-described "privately owned" buses violate the Fourteenth Amendment of the U.S. Constitution?

On June 19, 1956, a three-judge panel ruled that Montgomery's segregation codes "deny and deprive plaintiffs and other Negro citizens similarly situated of the equal protection of the laws and due process of law secured by the Fourteenth Amendment."[9] The court based their *Browder* decision on the precedent of the 1954 *Brown v. Board of Education of Topeka, Kansas* ruling. In that case, the U.S. Supreme Court ruled that "separate but equal" schools are inherently unequal and therefore unconstitutional.

The circuit court's decision was immediately appealed by the city's lawyers, paving the way for a showdown before the U.S. Supreme Court. In November 1956, the nation's high court found that

Parks worked closely with Martin Luther King Jr. during the Montgomery bus boycott and other protests.

E.D. Nixon escorts Parks to the courthouse on March 19, 1956. While the courts were wrangling with Browder v. Gale, Montgomery officials placed Nixon, Parks, King, and other civil rights leaders on trial for holding a boycott. King had to pay a fine; the others did not.

Montgomery's segregation policies, like Topeka's school policies, were unconstitutional. Segregation had finally been effectively outlawed.

Parks remembered the moment she heard news of the court's decision. "We were having one of our mass meetings at the time," she recalled. "Montgomery officials were going to break up the caucus we had and arrest many of the people in their cars in the car pool. We were very glad to know that the United States Supreme Court had made the ruling."[10]

As word of the ruling spread, the black community of Montgomery erupted in victorious joy, and 381 days after it started, the bus boycott

The bus boycott lasted from December 1955 to November 1956, when the Supreme Court ruled that Montgomery's bus segregation policy was unconstitutional. The ruling came just as city officials were going to try to break the boycott by arresting members of car pools.

ended. For Rosa, it was a social turning point. "I was glad that the type of treatment—legally enforced segregation—on the buses was over . . . had come to an end. It was something rather special."[11]

Parks also knew the real battle had just begun. It was one thing to change the law, but quite another to change attitudes.

Dr. Martin Luther King Jr.

Civil rights leader Martin Luther King Jr. was born in Atlanta, Georgia, on January 15, 1929. Like his father and grandfather before him, Martin worked as a church pastor. In 1954, when he was just twenty-five, King was named pastor of the Dexter Avenue Baptist Church in Montgomery, Alabama, and became a member of the NAACP. Passionate and committed, King was ready to lead America's first great nonviolent civil rights demonstration: the bus boycott. During the boycott, King was harassed by local authorities and arrested by police, and his house was firebombed. By the time the boycott ended, he had emerged as a charismatic, articulate leader.

In 1957, King helped found and was elected president of the Southern Christian Leadership Conference (SCLC), which had been formed to spearhead the civil rights movement. Over the next eleven years, he wrote five books and traveled over six million miles to preach racial equality and denounce racism and hatred the world over.

King also organized many demonstrations, including one in Birmingham, Alabama, and a march on Washington, D.C., where he delivered his "I have a dream" speech. He was arrested nearly twenty times on charges related to civil disobedience, and was named *Time* magazine's Man of the Year in 1963. When he was thirty-five, he became the youngest man ever to receive the Nobel Peace Prize. His dedication to peace, equality, and human dignity made him not just an American civil rights figure, but also a respected global leader.

King receives the Nobel Peace Prize

On April 4, 1968, King was in Memphis, Tennessee, to support striking garbage workers. While standing on the balcony of his motel, he was assassinated by a single gun-shot. Five days later, President Lyndon B. Johnson declared a national day of mourning, and King was buried in Atlanta at the Ebenezer Baptist Church.

After the Supreme Court ruling, Rosa
Parks continued to work for civil rights.

CHAPTER
5

Legacy

Rosa Parks had led the way to an important legal victory, but it came at a high price. Her inability to find steady work, the stress of being the target of hatred, and internal disagreements between King and Montgomery's other civil rights leaders convinced Rosa and Raymond to leave Alabama in 1957 and move to Hampton, Virginia. Rosa was hired as a hostess in an inn located at Hampton Institute, but their stay was short. In August, Raymond, Rosa, and Leona moved to Detroit at the urging of Rosa's brother, Sylvester, and lived at his house. Rosa found work as a seamstress and settled down to live a relatively anonymous life. She and Raymond never had children, nor did they ever own a home. But they continued to be social activists, working whatever jobs they could find to support themselves. They also remained active in their community. In 1964, Rosa became a deaconess in the African Methodist Episcopal Church.

In the mid-1960s, Parks met John Conyers Jr. when he was campaigning for Michigan's First District congressional seat. He won the election, and she joined his staff as an assistant in March 1965. She worked for Congressman Conyers for twenty-three years, until she retired in 1988.

One of the highlights of Rosa Parks's life was participating in the 1963 March on Washington led by Martin Luther King Jr. She and other female civil rights activists were introduced to the crowd,

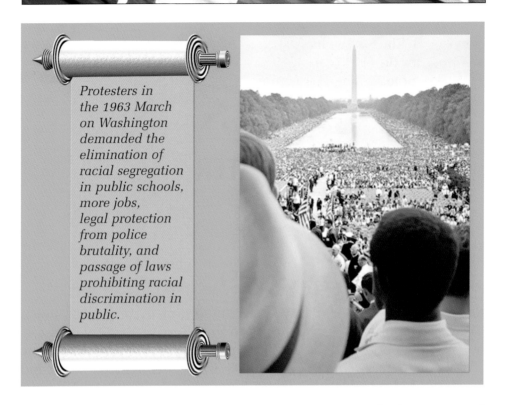

Protesters in the 1963 March on Washington demanded the elimination of racial segregation in public schools, more jobs, legal protection from police brutality, and passage of laws prohibiting racial discrimination in public.

estimated at a half million people. The march, which supported federal civil rights legislation, was the largest political demonstration in U.S. history up to that time.

"There were many people there," she recalled. "It was a great day for us. We were always hoping that there would be a civil rights bill passed in Washington. We always lived in hope that it would be a better day than what we lived in. I guess it took a long time because Congress and many of the people in House and Senate positions did not agree with our cause."[1]

A year later, the U.S. Congress passed the Civil Rights Act of 1964. The landmark legislation outlawed segregation in all American schools and public places. While originally intended to protect black citizens, the bill was eventually amended to include women and whites. The Civil Rights Act also established the Equal Employment Opportunity Commission, which protects employees in the workplace.

Ten years after Raymond's death from cancer in 1977, Rosa and her friend Elaine Steele cofounded the Rosa and Raymond Parks Institute for Self-Development in honor of Raymond. The institute's web site notes: "The Rosa and Raymond Parks Institute for Self-Development was named in honor of Raymond Parks because of his civil rights activism, his love for children and Mrs. Parks' love for him."[2]

The mandate of the organization is to motivate young people to reach their potential. Rosa Parks believed young people have the power to change the world, so she spent much of her later years talking at high schools, colleges, and other youth organizations.

"I always encourage children to stay in school, get good grades, and to believe in themselves," Rosa said. "Of course they should take care of their health and keep themselves from certain things that would be detrimental to them, either physically or mentally. They should be sure to get the best education that they can and choose careers that they can be progressive in as they go into their adulthood. . . . I urge children to have a spiritual awareness in their lives. If children work towards a positive goal in life, it will help them be successful when they become adults."[3]

One of the special programs the institute hosts is a summer road trip called Pathways to Freedom. Participating children and their chaperones tour the country in buses to follow the route of the Underground Railroad. They also visit places where important events of the civil rights movement, and the history of the country, occurred. Rosa accompanied the children for the first ten summers of the program.

"Mrs. Parks is a role model that these students look up to, and they feel very honored and privileged to be in her company," noted Steele. "And she's very gracious to accompany the students to these activities."[4]

Parks added, "We don't have enough young people who are concerned and who are exposed to the civil rights movement, and I would like to see more exposure and get their interest. . . . We give [young people] opportunities to meet many civil rights leaders. We teach them to be good citizens and do what they can do to help other people as they become successful themselves."[5]

Parks, who continued to work for social justice, marches with Representative Mickey Lelan of Texas at the South African Embassy in Washington, D.C. The December 1984 march protested South Africa's policies supporting apartheid, or racial segregation. In 1990, apartheid was abolished there.

Rosa stressed that the institute accepts young people of any race. "We don't discriminate against anyone. We teach people to reach their highest potential. I set examples by the way I lead my life."[6]

Although she became more physically frail with age, Rosa never lost her courage. In 1994, when she was eighty-one, Parks was attacked in her home by a burglar. Joseph Skipper, an admitted drug addict, acknowledged that he recognized Rosa, but still demanded money and struck her in the face before fleeing. After he was apprehended, he confessed and was sentenced to prison. Rosa later commented, "I pray for this young man and the conditions in our country that have made him this way. Despite the violence and crime in our society, we should not let fear overwhelm us. We must remain strong."[7]

In her later years, Rosa lived a quiet life, spending the winters in Los Angeles and the rest of the year in Detroit. She passed her days going to church, reading mail, and visiting patients in hospitals.

Although she was at peace with her life, she stopped short of saying she was happy.

"I do the very best I can to look upon life with optimism and hope and looking forward to a better day, but I don't think there is any such thing as complete happiness," she noted. "It pains me that there is still a lot of Klan activity and racism. I think when you say you're happy, you have everything that you need and everything that you want, and nothing more to wish for. I haven't reached that stage yet."[8]

Despite making tremendous gains toward equality, Parks felt America still had a long way to go in improving its race relations. "People need to free their minds of racial prejudice and believe in equality for all and freedom regardless of race," she said. "We need much more education—especially those who are narrow-minded. We need as much financial security as we can get. I think it would be a good thing if all people were treated equally and justly and not

In September 1996, President Bill Clinton presented Parks with the Presidential Medal of Freedom, one of many honors she received for her activism.

be discriminated against because of race or religion or anything that makes them different from others."[9]

As the new millennium approached and people looked back on the past 100 years of American history, there was a new appreciation for Rosa Parks and the part she played in the civil rights movement. In September 1996, President Bill Clinton presented Parks with the Presidential Medal of Freedom, the highest governmental award given to a nonmilitary citizen. She attended Clinton's January 1999 State of the Union address and received a standing ovation when acknowledged by the president. Six months later, Congress awarded Rosa the Congressional Gold Medal. Others honored that day were the American Red Cross, George Washington, and South African civil rights leader Nelson Mandela.

Among the hundreds of accolades she received during her lifetime was being voted by *Time* magazine as one of the 100 most influential people of the twentieth century. In a tribute to Parks, U.S. poet laureate Rita Dove noted, "At the end of this millennium (and a particularly noisy century), it is the modesty of Rosa Parks' example that sustains us. It is no less than the belief in the power of the individual, that cornerstone of the American Dream that she inspires, along with the hope that all of us—even the least of us—could be that brave, that serenely human, when crunch time comes."[10]

When asked how she felt about being called the mother of the civil rights movement, Parks usually responded by saying, "If people think of me in that way, I just accept the honor and appreciate it." In her book *Quiet Strength*, though, Rosa insisted that she did not change things alone. "Four decades later I am still uncomfortable with the credit given to me for starting the bus boycott. I would like [people] to know I was not the only person involved. I was just one of many who fought for freedom."[11]

Rosa Parks died on October 24, 2005, at the age of ninety-two. For two days, her casket was placed in the rotunda of the United States Capitol so that the public could pay its final respects. The woman who was once asked to vacate her seat on a bus became the first woman in American history to be laid in state at the Capitol, an honor usually reserved for U.S. presidents.

Irene Morgan Kirkaldy

Rosa Parks's arrest turned her into a national civil rights icon. But more than a decade before Parks made history, Irene Morgan Kirkaldy's refusal to give up her bus seat in Virginia led to a precedent-setting Supreme Court ruling banning segregation on interstate transportation.

Irene Kirkaldy

Irene was twenty-seven years old in July 1944 when she boarded a Greyhound bus in Gloucester, Virginia, for Baltimore, Maryland. A mother of two, Kirkaldy was recovering from a miscarriage and was on her way home to see her doctor. She sat in the section reserved for "colored" people, near the back of the bus. Next to her was a young woman holding her baby.

A half hour into the trip, a white couple boarded. The driver told Irene and the young mother to move farther back. Kirkaldy declined and insisted the other woman not move either.

"I didn't do anything wrong. I'd paid for my seat. I was sitting where I was supposed to. . . . Why should I move?"[12] she recalled.

The driver drove to the Saluda, Virginia, jail. When a sheriff boarded the bus to arrest her, Irene tore up the arrest warrant and kicked the sheriff in the groin. A second deputy dragged her off the bus and put her behind bars. At the trial, her attorney used a unique strategy. Instead of claiming segregation laws violated the Fourteenth Amendment, he argued that segregation laws unfairly impacted interstate commerce. That strategy failed, and Kirkaldy was found guilty and fined $10.

However, two young NAACP lawyers, future Supreme Court Justice Thurgood Marshall and William H. Hastie, appealed the decision all the way to the Supreme Court. On June 3, 1946, the Court ruled segregation in interstate transportation was an undue burden on commerce. Despite its importance, the case received little media or public attention, but it paved the way for Parks's actions a decade later.

In 2001, President Bill Clinton awarded Irene Kirkaldy the Presidential Citizens Medal—the second-highest civilian honor in the United States.

For Your Information

Chronology

1913	Rosa Louise McCauley is born February 4 in Tuskegee, Alabama.
1915	Her brother, Sylvester, is born.
1924	Rosa enrolls at Montgomery Industrial School for Girls.
1932	She marries Raymond Parks.
1934	She earns her high school diploma.
1943	Rosa joins the NAACP in December.
1955	On December 1, she is arrested for not giving up her bus seat for a white passenger. She is found guilty on December 5, so her lawyers appeal her case.
1957	Rosa and Raymond move to Detroit.
1964	Rosa becomes a deaconess in the AME Church.
1965	She begins working in the office of Congressman John Conyers Jr.
1977	Raymond dies; so does Sylvester.
1987	With Elaine Steele, Rosa founds the Rosa and Raymond Parks Institute for Self-Development.
1988	Rosa retires from working with Congressman Conyers.
1996	Rosa is awarded the Presidential Medal of Freedom.
1997	Michigan designates the first Monday following February 4 as Rosa Parks Day; she becomes the first living person to be honored with a holiday.
1998	Ground is broken in Montgomery for the Rosa Parks Museum and Library.
1999	Rosa attends the State of the Union address and receives a standing ovation; she is awarded the Congressional Gold Medal.
2000	Rosa meets Pope John Paul II in St. Louis, Missouri.
2002	CBS airs TV movie *The Rosa Parks Story* on February 24.
2005	Rosa dies October 24; she becomes the first woman in American history to be laid in state in the U.S. Capitol.

Timeline in History

1863 Emancipation Proclamation takes the first step in freeing all slaves in the United States.

1865 Abraham Lincoln is assassinated on April 14 by Confederate sympathizer John Wilkes Booth.

1868 The Fourteenth Amendment is ratified.

1925 Texas passes legislation requiring schools to be segregated.

1945 First Nuremberg trial for Nazi war crimes begins.

1948 Malcolm Little, who will one day be known as civil rights leader Malcolm X, is introduced to the Nation of Islam by his brother.

1955 Emmett Till is murdered in Mississippi.

1957 On an order from the Arkansas governor, nine black students are prevented from entering Little Rock's Central High School.

1961 Amnesty International is formed.

1962 James Meredith becomes the first black student to enroll at the University of Mississippi; Cesar Chavez forms the United Farm Workers of America.

1963 Martin Luther King Jr. writes "Letter from Birmingham Jail."

1964 Three civil rights workers are murdered in Mississippi; President Lyndon B. Johnson signs Civil Rights Act, which gives all people equal access to public places and outlaws job discrimination; Martin Luther King Jr. receives the Nobel Peace Prize.

1965 Jimmie Lee Jackson is murdered near Selma, Alabama, prompting a series of historic civil rights protests.

1968 Soviet tanks invade Prague, Czechoslovakia, to crush the democratic movement there; Martin Luther King Jr. is assassinated.

1971 The Supreme Court upholds busing to achieve integration.

1982 Bryant Gumbel is the first African American to anchor a national news program, on NBC.

1991 President George H. W. Bush signs a new civil rights act, which is aimed primarily at gender discrimination.

1993 Nelson Mandela receives the Nobel Peace Prize for his work in integrating South Africa.

1998 U.S. Congress passes the Hate Crimes Prevention Act.

2007 Former Alabama state trooper James Bonard Fowler is indicted for the 1965 murder of Jimmie Lee Jackson.

2008 Senator Edward Kennedy of Massachusetts and Representative John Lewis of Georgia propose a new civil rights act, which would ensure federal money is not used to support discriminatory practices and would strengthen laws against age discrimination.

Chapter Notes

Chapter One. Tired

1 William Bradford Huie, *Killers' Confession,* http://www.pbs.org/wgbh/amex/till/sfeature/sf_look.html
2. Ibid.
3. Ibid.

Chapter Two. Growing Up Segregated

1. Académie Clermont-Ferrand, "Rosa Parks: The Interview," http://www3.ac-clermont.fr/pedago/anglaislp/ressources/dossiers/rosa_2.htm
2. Ibid.
3. Rosa Parks, "Commentary of a Black Southern Bus Rider," interview by Sidney Roger (Los Angeles, 1962), http://www.PacificaRadioArchives.org
4. Macomb County Bar Association, *Interview of the Month,* "Rosa Parks by Charlie Langton," http://www.macombbar.org/displaycommon.cfm?an=1&subarticlenbr=155
5. Academy of Achievement, *Rosa Parks,* "Rosa Parks Interview," http://www.achievement.org/autodoc/page/par0int-1
6. Academy of Achievement, *Rosa Parks,* "Rosa Parks Biography," http://www.achievement.org/autodoc/page/par0bio-1
7. Academy of Achievement, *Rosa Parks,* "Rosa Parks Interview."
8. Academy of Achievement, *Rosa Parks,* "Rosa Parks Biography."
9. Ibid.
10. Kira Albin, "Rosa Parks: The Woman Who Changed a Nation," http://www.grandtimes.com/rosa.html

Chapter Three. Birth of an Activist

1. Democracy Now!, "Rosa Parks 1913–2005: We Air a Rare 1956 Interview with Parks During the Montgomery Bus Boycott," http://www.democracynow.org/article.pl?sid=05/10/25/1412239#transcript
2. Kira Albin, "Rosa Parks: The Woman Who Changed a Nation," http://www.grandtimes.com/rosa.html

3. Rita Dove, "The Torchbearer," *Time,* June 14, 1999, http://www.time.com/time/magazine/article/0,9171,991252-2,00.html
4. Rita Dove, "Rosa Parks," http://www.time.com/time/time100/heroes/profile/parks01.html
5. Ibid.
6. Macomb County Bar Association, *Interview of the Month,* "Rosa Parks by Charlie Langton," http://www.macombbar.org/displaycommon.cfm?an=1&subarticlenbr=155
7. Dove "The Torchbearer."
8. Ibid.
9. Democracy Now!
10. National Park Service, *14th Amendment to the U.S. Constitution,* http://www.nps.gov/archive/malu/documents/amend14.htm
11. The National Center for Public Policy Research, *Brown v. Board of Education,* http://www.nationalcenter.org/brown.html

Chapter Four. Fallout

1. Democracy Now!, "Rosa Parks 1913–2005: We Air a Rare 1956 Interview with Parks During the Montgomery Bus Boycott," http://www.democracynow.org/article.pl?sid=05/10/25/1412239#transcript
2. Ibid.
3. Académie Clermont-Ferrand, "Rosa Parks: The Interview," http://www3.ac-clermont.fr/pedago/anglaislp/ressources/dossiers/rosa_2.htm
4. Ibid.
5. Democracy Now!
6. Kira Albin, "Rosa Parks: The Woman Who Changed a Nation," http://www.grandtimes.com/rosa.html
7. "Interview with Rosa Parks," http://teacher.scholastic.com/rosa/interview.htm
8. Academy of Achievement, *Rosa Parks,* "Rosa Parks Interview," http://www.achievement.org/autodoc/page/par0int-1

9. Tolerance.org, *Tolerance in the News,* "Remembering Rosa Parks: 1913–2005," http://www.tolerance.org/news/article_tol.jsp?id=1319
10. Macomb County Bar Association, *Interview of the Month,* "Rosa Parks by Charlie Langton," http://www.macombbar.org/displaycommon.cfm?an=1&subarticlenbr=155
11. Democracy Now!

Chapter Five. Legacy
1. Macomb County Bar Association, *Interview of the Month,* "Rosa Parks by Charlie Langton," http://www.macombbar.org/displaycommon.cfm?an=1&subarticlenbr=155
2. Rosa & Raymond Parks Institute for Self-Development, "Did You Know?," http://www.rosaparks.org/dyk
3. Democracy Now!, "Rosa Parks 1913–2005: We Air a Rare 1956 Interview with Parks During the Montgomery Bus Boycott," http://www.democracynow.org/article.pl?sid=05/10/25/1412239#transcript
4. Kira Albin, "Rosa Parks: The Woman Who Changed a Nation," http://www.grandtimes.com/rosa.html
5. Ibid.
6. Democracy Now!
7. Ibid.
8. Academy of Achievement, *Rosa Parks,* "Rosa Parks Biography," http://www.achievement.org/autodoc/page/par0bio-1
9. Democracy Now!
10. Rita Dove, "Rosa Parks," http://www.time.com/time/time100/heroes/profile/parks01.html
11. Albin.
12. Yvonne Shinhoster Lamb, "Irene M. Kirkaldy; Case Spurred Freedom Rides," *Washington Post,* August 13, 2007, p. B04.

Further Reading

For Young Adults
Edwards, Pamela Duncan. *The Bus Ride That Changed History: The Story of Rosa Parks.* Illustrated by Danny Shanahan. New York: Houghton Mifflin, 2005.
Parks, Rosa, and Jim Haskins. *Rosa Parks: My Story.* New York: Scholastic, 1992.
Parks, Rosa, and Gregory J. Reed. *Dear Mrs. Parks: A Dialogue with Today's Youth.* New York: Lee & Low Books, 1996.
Parks, Rosa, and Gregory J. Reed. *Quiet Strength: The Faith, the Hope, and the Heart of a Woman Who Changed a Nation.* Grand Rapids, Michigan: Zondervan, 1994.

Works Consulted
Branch, Taylor. *Parting the Waters: America in the King Years 1954–63.* New York: Simon & Schuster, 1988.
Burns, Stewart, ed. *Daybreak of Freedom: The Montgomery Bus Boycott.* Chapel Hill, North Carolina: University of North Carolina Press, 1997.
Dimitriadis, Greg, and Dennis Carlson, eds. *Promises to Keep: Cultural Studies, Democratic Education, and Public Life.* New York: RoutledgeFalmer, 2003.
Hardy, Gayle J. *American Women Civil Rights Activists: Biobibliographies of 68 Leaders, 1825–1992.* Jefferson, North Carolina: McFarland, 1993.
Hine, Darlene Clark, Elsa Barkley Brown, and Rosalyn Terborg-Penn, eds. *Black Women in America: An Historical Encyclopedia.* 2 vols. Brooklyn, New York: Carlson Publishing, 1993.
Lamb, Yvonne Shinhoster. "Irene M. Kirkaldy; Case Spurred Freedom Rides." *Washington Post,* August 13, 2007.

Levy, Peter B. *The Civil Rights Movement.* Westport, Connecticut: Greenwood Press, 1998.

Peake, Thomas R. *Keeping the Dream Alive: A History of the Southern Christian Leadership Conference from King to the Nineteen Eighties.* New York: Peter Lang, 1987.

Scholastic: *Rosa Parks: How I Fought for Civil Rights*
http://teacher.scholastic.com/rosa/index.htm

Shipp, E. R. "Rosa Parks, 92, Founding Symbol of Civil Rights Movement, Dies"
http://www.nytimes.com/2005/10/25/national/25parks.html?_r=1&oref=slogin

On the Internet

Académie Clermont-Ferrand: "Rosa Parks: The Interview"
http://www3.ac-clermont.fr/pedago/anglaislp/ressources/dossiers/rosa_2.htm

Academy of Achievement: Rosa Parks, "Rosa Parks Biography"
http://www.achievement.org/autodoc/page/par0bio-1

Academy of Achievement: Rosa Parks, "Rosa Parks Interview"
http://www.achievement.org/autodoc/page/par0int-1

Albin, Kira. "Rosa Parks: The Woman Who Changed a Nation"
http://www.grandtimes.com/rosa.html

Democracy Now!: "Rosa Parks 1913–2005: We Air a Rare 1956 Interview with Parks During the Montgomery Bus Boycott"
http://www.democracynow.org/article.pl?sid=05/10/25/1412239#transcript

Dove, Rita. "Rosa Parks." *Time.* June 14, 1999.
http://www.time.com/time/time100/heroes/profile/parks01.html

Dove, Rita. "The Torchbearer." *Time.* June 14, 1999.
http://www.time.com/time/magazine/article/0,9171,991252-1,00.html

Huie, William Bradford. *Killers' Confession.*
http://www.pbs.org/wgbh/amex/till/sfeature/sf_look.html

Macomb County Bar Association: Interview of the Month, "Rosa Parks by Charlie Langton"
http://www.macombbar.org/displaycommon.cfm?an=1&subarticlenbr=155

The National Center for Public Policy Research: *Brown v. Board of Education*
http://www.nationalcenter.org/brown.html

National Park Service: *14th Amendment to the U.S. Constitution.*
http://www.nps.gov/archive/malu/documents/amend14.htm

Parks, Rosa. "Commentary of a Black Southern Bus Rider." Interview by Sidney Roger. (Los Angeles, 1962). http://www.PacificaRadioArchives.org

Rosa & Raymond Parks Institute for Self-Development
http://www.rosaparks.org

Tolerance.org: Tolerance in the News, "Remembering Rosa Parks: 1913–2005"
http://www.tolerance.org/news/article_tol.jsp?id=1319

Glossary

bigotry (BIH-guh-tree)
Intolerance of others based on skin color or ethnicity.

boycott (BOY-kot)
To stop using a product of service out of protest.

carpetbaggers (KAR-pet-BAA-gurs)
Northerners who moved down South to make money from post–Civil War rebuilding.

caucus (KAW-kuss)
A closed meeting.

flog (FLOG)
To beat or strike with a whip.

indictment (in-DYT-ment)
An official charge for committing a crime.

loiter (LOY-tur)
To linger in the same spot.

lynched (LINCHT)
Hanged by a mob.

peonage (PEE-uh-nihj)
Having to work for a creditor until a debt is paid off.

poet laureate (POH-et LAH-ree-et)
A government-appointed poet who composes poems for State occasions and other government events.

segregation (seh-greh-GAY-shun)
Separating people because of race, gender, or ethnic background.

Index